SACRAMENTO PUBLIC LIBRARY
D0535134

Count them while you can…

With love, to my mother, Margaret, my husband, Norman and my children, Jonathan and Elisabeth.

To the memory of Tony Oliver and with thanks to Carol.

Little Hare Books
8/21 Mary Street, Surry Hills
NSW 2010 AUSTRALIA

www.littleharebooks.com

First published 2010

National Library of Australia
Cataloguing-in-Publication entry

Bowman, Anne.
Count them while you can/Anne Bowman.
978 1 921541 60 5 (hbk.)
For primary school age.
Endangered species - Juvenile literature.
Animals - Infancy - Juvenile literature.

591.68

Designed by Lore Foye
Produced by Pica Digital, Singapore
Printed through Phoenix Offset
Printed in Shen Zhen, Guangdong Province, China, March 2010

5 4 3 2 1

ANNE BOWMAN

COUNT THEM WHILE YOU CAN ...

Leadbeater's Possum

GYMNOBELIDEUS LEADBEATERI

In the mountain ash forest,
on a silvery gum,
lived a Leadbeater's possum
with her baby possum, one.
'Cling!' said the mother.
'I cling!' said the one.
So they climbed and they clung
on the silvery gum.

HABITAT:	Central Highlands of Victoria, Australia, above 500 m, mainly in mountain ash forests.
SIZE:	Up to 140 g in weight, and 32 cm long, including 16 cm tail.
YOUNG:	1 – 2 babies. Pouch life of about 85 days. Weaned at 10 – 15 months old.
FOOD:	Insects, tree sap.
THREATS:	Habitat loss from logging and fires.
NUMBER LEFT:	Less than 1000 in the wild. None captive (2009).

Guam Micronesian Kingfisher

TODIRAMPHUS CINNAMOMINUS CINNAMOMINUS

On a tropical island,
where the gentle winds blew,
lived a pair of kingfishers
and their noisy babies, two.
'Eat!' said the parents.
'We eat!' said the two.
So they ate and they grew
where the gentle winds blew.

HABITAT:	Lived mainly in mature forests, mixed woodland and second-growth forest of the Pacific island of Guam.
SIZE:	Up to 74 g in weight, and 24 cm long.
YOUNG:	1 – 3 babies. Nest in hole in a tree or in termite nest. Babies leave nest at about 35 days.
FOOD:	Crabs, lizards, insects.
THREATS:	The introduced brown tree snake.
NUMBER LEFT:	Extinct in the wild. 113 captive (2009).

Kakapo

STRIGOPS HABROPTILA

Safe beneath the fern fronds,
near the base of a tree,
lived a kakapo mother
and her lively chicks, three.
'Scratch!' said the mother.
'We scratch!' said the three.
So they scratched and explored
near the base of the tree.

HABITAT:	New Zealand, offshore on protected islands.
SIZE:	Up to 3.5 kg in weight, and 60 cm long.
YOUNG:	1 – 4 babies. Nest under cover of plants, in a cavity at the base of a tree, or between rocks. Chicks leave nest at about 10 weeks. Fed by mother up to 6 months.
FOOD:	Roots, leaves, seeds, fruits, bulbs, flowers, cones, pollen.
THREATS:	Cats, weasels, rats and ferrets (introduced predators) on the mainland.
NUMBER LEFT:	124 on island reserves (2009).

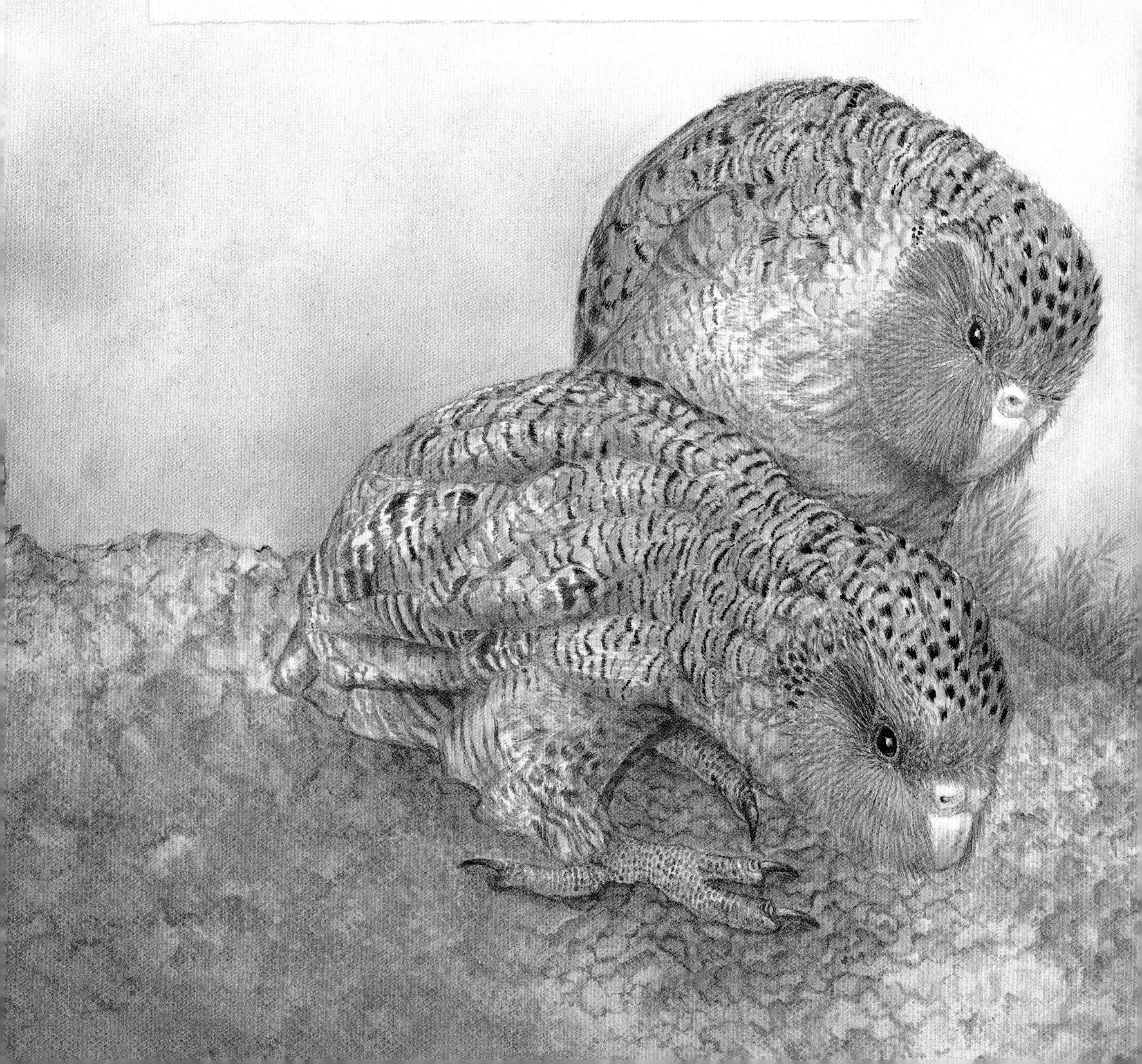

Numbat

MYRMECOBIUS FASCIATUS

Over in the woodland,
on the soft forest floor,
lived a stripy mother numbat
and her little numbats, four.
'Sniff!' said the mother.
'We sniff!' said the four.
So they sniffed and they scratched
on the soft forest floor.

HABITAT:	South-west Western Australia in eucalypt woodlands.
SIZE:	Up to 550 g in weight, and 45 cm long, including 22 – 23 cm tail.
YOUNG:	2 – 4 babies, carried around by the mother for the first six months. Left in a burrow after 6 months and suckled at night. Sometimes carried on mother's back when travelling. Independent at about 11 months.
FOOD:	Termites.
THREATS:	Habitat loss, foxes, native predators.
NUMBER LEFT:	Estimated to be less than 1000 adults, living in 9 wild populations and 6 free-ranging, fenced populations (2008).

Snow Leopard

PANTHERA UNCIA

In the snow-capped mountains,
where the strongest survive,
lived a mother snow leopard
and her fluffy cubs, five.
'Leap!' said the mother.
'We leap!' said the five.
So they leapt and they pounced
where the strongest survive.

HABITAT:	The high mountains of Central Asia and Northern India.
SIZE:	Up to 75 kg in weight, and 2.3 m long, including 100 cm tail.
YOUNG:	1 – 5 cubs. Nest lined with mother's fur. Suckling for 5 months, running and eating at 2 months. Cubs leave mother at about 18 months.
FOOD:	Wild sheep, goats, deer, boar, other small mammals, birds.
THREATS:	Illegal hunting.
NUMBER LEFT:	3000 – 7000 in the wild. 600 – 700 Captive (2009).

Red-Ruffed Lemur

VARECIA VARIEGATA RUBRA

In the lush rainforest,
near their nest made of sticks,
lived some red-ruffed lemurs
and their little lemurs, six.
'Climb!' said the mothers.
'We climb!' said the six.
So they clambered and climbed
near their nest made of sticks.

HABITAT:	Rainforests of Masoala Peninsula in Madagascar, Africa.
SIZE:	Up to 4 kg in weight, and 120 cm long, including 65 cm tail.
YOUNG:	1 – 6 young. Nest of sticks, leaves and fur. Babies begin to leave nest at around 3 weeks with mother or other relatives. Weaned about 4 – 5 months.
FOOD:	Fruit, leaves, shoots, seeds, nectar.
THREATS:	Habitat loss, hunting.
NUMBER LEFT:	Numbers decreasing. No current estimate of wild population. Over 200 captive (2009).

Black-Footed Ferret

MUSTELA NIGRIPES

Beneath the cold prairie,
where the winds never threaten,
lived a black-footed ferret
and her little kits, seven.
'Play!' said the mother.
'We play!' said the seven.
So they scampered and played
where the winds never threaten.

HABITAT:	Prairies of Wyoming and South Dakota, USA.
SIZE:	Up to 1000 g in weight, and 54 cm long, including 13 cm tail.
YOUNG:	1 – 7 kits. Shelter in prairie-dog burrows. Stay below ground until 2 months old. Leave home at about 8 months.
FOOD:	Main diet consists of prairie dogs. Also, ground squirrels, rodents, birds, rabbits.
THREATS:	Disappearance of prairie dogs due to habitat destruction, poisoning, hunting and disease.
NUMBER LEFT:	Approximately 1000 in the wild. 300 captive (2008).

Red-Breasted Goose

BRANTA RUFICOLLIS

Out on the tundra,
by a freshwater lake,
lived a pair of waddling geese
and their little goslings, eight.
'Swim!' said the parents.
'We swim!' said the eight.
So they swam and they paddled
on the freshwater lake.

HABITAT:	Breeds in Russia's Arctic tundra. Spends winters in Eastern Europe on farmland by lakes and the sea.
SIZE:	Up to 1.6 kg in weight, and 56 cm long.
YOUNG:	3 – 10 eggs. Nest on the ground, close to a peregrine falcon's nest for protection. Chicks fledge at 5 – 6 weeks.
FOOD:	Roots, seeds, leaves, shoots.
THREATS:	Habitat destruction, hunting.
NUMBER LEFT:	Estimated average of 37,000 in the wild, with numbers decreasing rapidly (2006).

Idaho Ground Squirrel

SPERMOPHILUS BRUNNEUS

Over in a meadow,
near a forest of pine,
lived a mother ground squirrel
and her baby squirrels, nine.
'Romp!' said the mother.
'We romp!' said the nine.
So they romped and they frolicked
near the forest of pine.

HABITAT:	West-central Idaho, USA, in grassy meadows surrounded by pine forests.
SIZE:	Up to 258 g in weight, depending on season, and up to 32 cm long, including 4.6 – 5 cm tail.
YOUNG:	1 – 10 young. Suckle for about 3 weeks. Emerge from burrow at about 50 days.
FOOD:	Grasses, leaves, seeds, flowers, bulbs.
THREATS:	Habitat loss, hunting, introduction of non-native grasses.
NUMBER LEFT:	1400 of northern subspecies and 4000 of southern subspecies in the wild (2008).

Californian Sea Otter

ENHYDRA LUTRIS NEREIS

In the billowing ocean,
where the kelp sways and bends,
lived some mother sea otters
and their fluffy kits, ten.
'Sleep!' said the mothers.
'We sleep!' said the ten.
So they slept and they basked
where the kelp sways and bends.

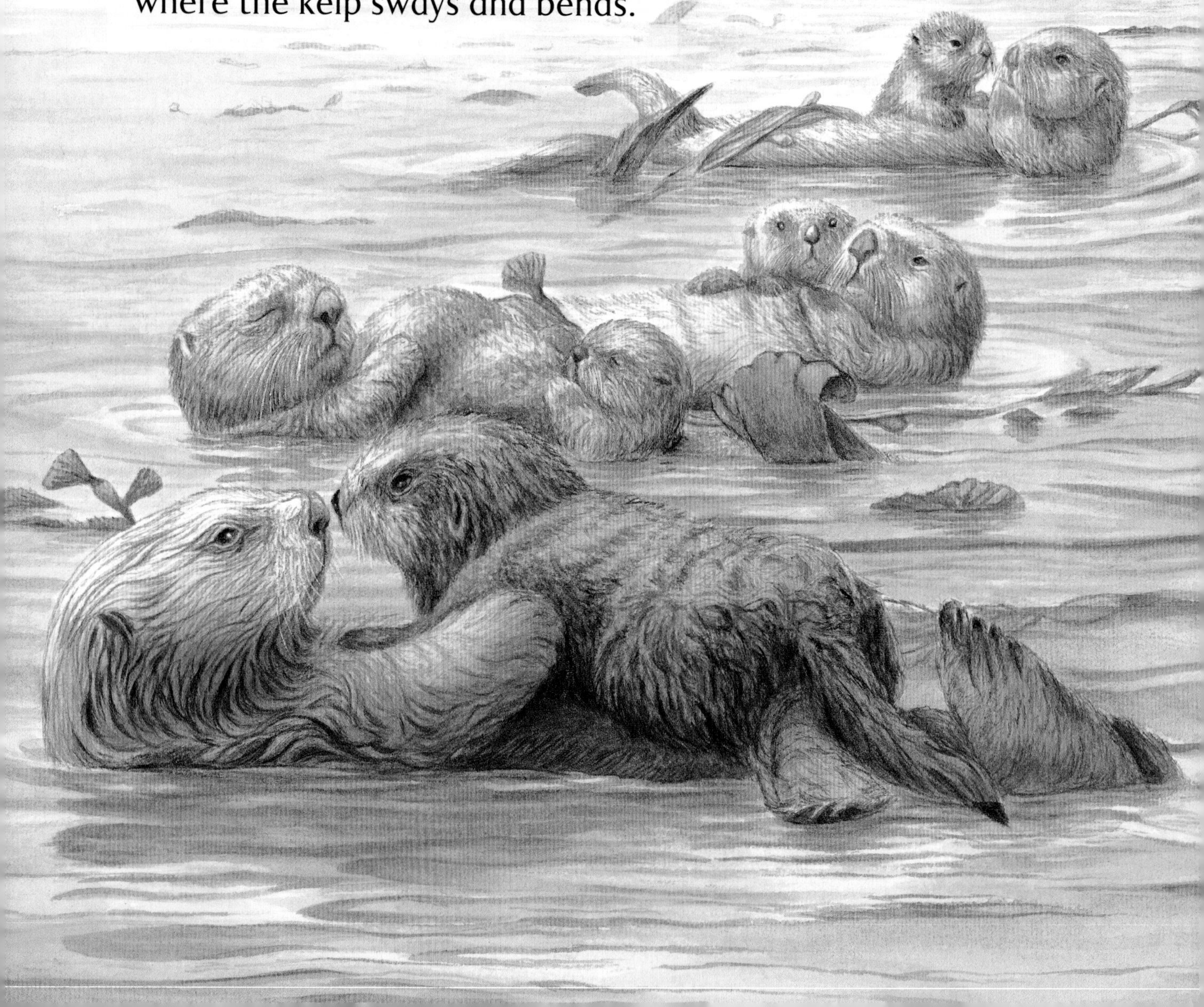

HABITAT:	Off the coast of central California, particularly kelp forests.
SIZE:	Up to 45 kg in weight, and 1.5 m long.
YOUNG:	Usually 1 pup. Suckles for 2 – 4 months. After 13 weeks, pup practises swimming and diving with mother. Independent from 6 months.
FOOD:	Sea urchins, molluscs, crustaceans, fish.
THREATS:	Oil spills, killer whales (orcas), fishing, illegal hunting, infectious disease. As many as 10,000 sea otters can be killed in a single oil spill.
NUMBER LEFT:	2654 in the wild (2009).

How do we know if a species is endangered?

Before an animal species is called endangered, scientists must study many things about it. These include:

- Counting the total number of animals left
- Counting the number of animals that are able to produce young
- Working out whether the number of animals has been falling and, if so, how fast and for how long
- Studying the habitat where the species lives
- Checking to see if there is any disease amongst the animals
- Working out if there are natural disturbances to the species and their habitat
- Working out if there are man-made disturbances to the habitat

Scientists then give the species a conservation status.

The list below tells you the different types of conservation status and what each of them means.

Extinct: Species in which the last animal has died

Extinct in the wild: Species that have no animals living in the wild, but do have animals surviving in captivity or in managed populations

Critically endangered: Species with an extremely high risk of extinction in the immediate future in the wild, or with an extremely high risk of becoming completely extinct in the immediate future

Endangered: Species threatened with extinction because there are so few of them left, and because their population is decreasing

Vulnerable: Species that may become endangered if the conditions that help them to survive and produce young do not get better

Near threatened: Species that are not in the high-risk categories but that could move into one of these in the near future

Least concern: Species that do not fit into the high-risk categories

Data deficient: Species about which there is not enough information for scientists to decide if they are at the risk of extinction

Not evaluated: Species that have not been assessed

Most of the animals in *Count Them While You Can* belong to the **endangered** category. The kakapo is **critically endangered** and the Guam Micronesian kingfisher is **extinct in the wild**.

Rhyming text can be sung to the tune of 'Over in the Meadow'.

Acknowledgements:

Dr Anne D. Yoder, Duke Lemur Center, NC, USA

Mr David Haring, Duke Lemur Center, NC, USA

Barbara Martinez PhD, University of Minnesota, USA

Dr Sandy Ingleby, Australian Museum, NSW, Australia

The Snow Leopard Trust, Seattle, WA, USA

Friends of Leadbeater's Possum Inc., Healesville, VIC, Australia

Kakapo Recovery Programme, Dept. of Conservation, New Zealand

Dr Ross Shegog PhD, Houston, TX, USA

Gillian McGrouther, Rochdale, Lancashire, England

Black-footed Ferret Recovery Implementation Team, Wellington, CO, USA

U.S. Fish and Wildlife Service, USA

IUCN Red List

The Mammals of Australia by R. Strahan (New Holland Publishers, 2008)